Lambs' Tales
from Great Operas

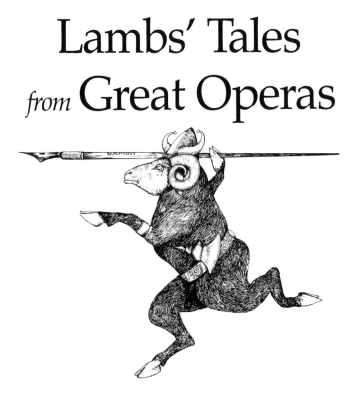

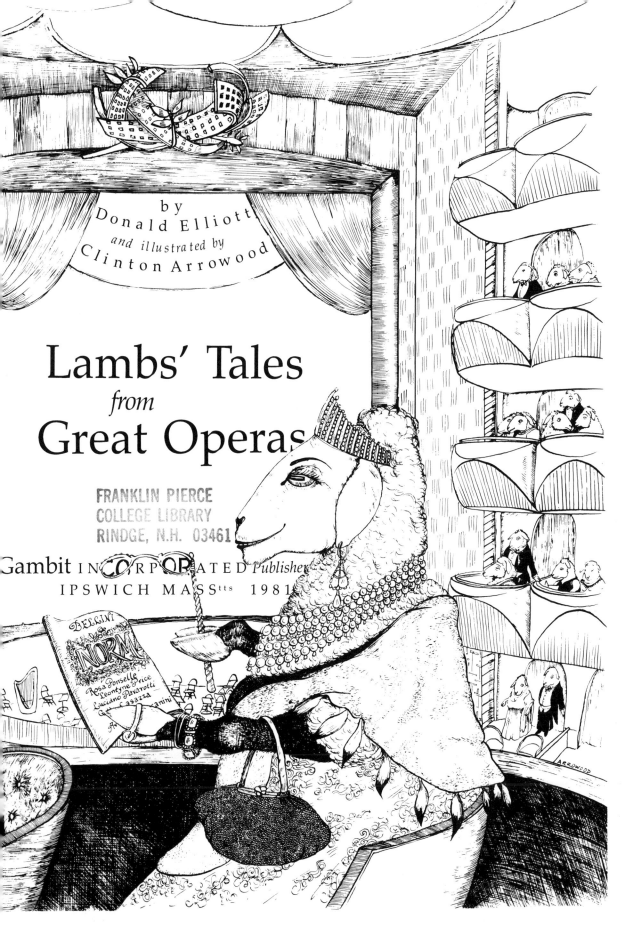

by
Donald Elliott
and illustrated by
Clinton Arrowood

Lambs' Tales
from
Great Operas

Gambit INCORPORATED Publisher
IPSWICH MASStts 1981

First Printing

Library of Congress Cataloging in Publication Data

Elliott, Donald.
  Lambs' Tales from Great Operas.

  I. Operas—Stories, plots, etc. I. Arrowood, Clinton.
  II. Title. III. Title: Tales from great operas.
MT95.E44   782.1'3   80-84719
ISBN 0-87645-110-5   AACR2

Contents

A Foreword

We will begin by speaking of oysters. Oysters, by their very natures, produce divisions among people. There are those who approach oysters with unrestrained enthusiasm, considering them to be supremely succulent examples of the Creator's basic concern for the well-being of humanity. There are those, on the other hand, who look upon them as rather horrid suggestions of the depths to which man will descend in his attempts at self-gratification. And then there are those who fall into neither category, approaching oysters rather warily, reluctantly persuaded, on the one hand, that there must be something to them that should not be missed but equally convinced, on the other hand, that there is something essentially absurd about them.

Opera, we think, is somewhat analogous. For the cognoscenti, that slightly singular breed, the opera lover, we offer a new visit to a few old operatic friends, a new approach, as it were, to the succulent oyster. For the operatically cautious, those who are a bit suspicious of what is really behind it all or who are healthily resistant to learning about opera, we tender a basically affectionate introduction, an invitation to savor the toothsome, if occasionally absurd, delights that lie waiting. Finally, for those who refuse not only tender intimacies with oysters or with opera, but who absolutely reject even a cursory acquaintance, we can only trust that for them there are other areas of human experience that afford rewards of equivalent value.

Only a fool or a very wise man would attempt to present any kind of final, definitive, or even very original exposition of opera, for it is very possibly the most voluminous, convoluted, and well-nigh overwhelming form of artistic expression yet conceived by the mind and soul of man. We know we are not wise, and we hope we are not fools, so we will attempt only to proffer a few observations about opera such as might be made by one occupying a position somewhere between those extremes.

Opera is, usually, absolutely spectacular. A great part of its appeal, as a matter of fact, lies in its sheer spectacle. And what boundless resources it has to draw upon! For opera combines music—both instrumental and that of the human voice—with words, with acting, with dramatic plots—often highly emotional and charged with theatrical tension—with sets, lights, and stage effects, and, curiously somehow, with a kind of audience participation that it reserves particularly for itself. Opera is, to a greater or lesser degree, fashionable, and has probably always been so. One "dresses" for opera, usually; minks and diamonds and royalty and nobility and "class" abound. Perhaps this is somewhat less so today, particularly with the emergence and popularity of the American "musical," which could with a bit of stretching be considered a form of opera; but in a very real sense the compass of opera, specifically "grand opera," includes the character of its audiences. There have always, of course, been "light" operas—operettas, musical comedies—which have offered a somewhat broader appeal, and there have always been audiences of the common folk, but the truly grandiose forms of opera are usually more closely associated, at least in the general public mind, with the grandes dames of society and their slightly stuffy husbands—complete, on occasion, with hearing aids that can be turned off—than with the basically impecunious elements of the citizenry.

The historical progression of the operatic form is complex and involved. As is the case with the development of most artistic creations, opera has moved through phases, periods, and highly varied stages of growth. In a sense, Greek drama, with the declamations of the chorus, often with a fairly rudimentary musical accompaniment—at least in comparison to the music of the West—could be considered as being the beginning of opera. But the first examples of the form that culminated in what today we call opera probably occurred at about the turn of the seventeenth century, and, in a manner somewhat parallel to the growth of the drama, had their genesis in the miracle plays, themselves outgrowths of the liturgical drama of the Christian church.

But what, really, *is* opera? Essentially it is a combination, a fusion, of separate elements that could conceivably stand by themselves on their own merits. The dramatic portions, that is, the plots that unfold on the stage, involve the tragedies of unrequited love, the fateful consequences of human error and misunderstanding, the bitter wages of sin, the confrontations of men and gods, and innumerable other agonies and ecstasies of the human spirit. The musical parts of operas are themselves combinations of instrumental sound with that of the human voice, blending together with each other as well as with the dramatic action and the distinguishing features of the characters. Opera is, then, a lyric stage performance that utilizes music, plot, and sets to produce a unified effect that transcends its individual parts.

Early opera, in the seventeenth century, followed to a large extent the recitative style, in which the dramatic utterances of a singer were presented on a background that was a more or less unmelodic and spare accompaniment. Later in that century, however, opera became less concerned with plot and dramatic intensity than it was with melody and with being a means for the showing off of singers' voices, and for a time it followed this tradition, offering in some instances little more than an opportunity for singers to don costumes and rattle the rafters of the local concert halls with the power of their voices. With the advent of Gluck in the eighteenth century, however, opera achieved a more complete and balanced combination of music and drama, and it moved considerably closer to the form that most of us today consider as essentially operatic. The Romantic movement of the late eighteenth and early nineteenth centuries, echoed in virtually all artistic creativity of the period, affected the opera profoundly, and it was this era that ushered in the great contributions of Mozart, Beethoven, Rossini, Donizetti, and a host of others. And in the late nineteenth century until our own time, opera—again like so much in the realms of literature and art—moved to a realism that cast off embellishments and what were often exaggerated sentiments, a movement that gave way to impressionism and, eventually, to our modern experimental forms that disdain "accepted" conventions.

Besides the various forms that opera has taken over the centuries, it has also been intimately associated with the progress of social change and with the character of regional background. While Italy is probably more closely associated with the form than any other country, opera has flourished in and been influenced by many other nationalities, notably France, Germany, England, Russia, and the United States. One result of this varied background is and has always been the problem of language. Although art may be in many senses a universal language, the fact remains that operas are written in a specific language that is set to music, and it is rare, if not impossible, to find translated versions that do not somehow lose something essential through the mere process of translation. On the other hand, the nature of opera is such that it often seems not particularly necessary to understand all the words, as long as one has some idea of approximately what is going on and can feel the meaning that underlies the entire structure. Actually, if an exact understanding of the words is, indeed, necessary to get anything from an opera, perhaps it could be concluded either that a listener is a bit blind to a grander view of things or that the opera itself doesn't really *have* a grander view. While one may, for example, not understand precisely what Carmen is saying in so many words, it would be a rather obtuse individual who didn't understand what she really means or wants or is offering.

While man, ever since he has been man, has wandered about his world with the vague but persistent question mark hovering over his head as to the purpose of his existence, it could be suggested that whatever that purpose is, it has something to do with communication. His understanding, a product of reasoning, depends, nonetheless, on impressions delivered basically through his senses, and his interpretation of those impressions constitutes his rather desperate attempts to establish some sort of communication with everything outside himself. But all these impressions come to him in the form of symbols, for he can never really take into his mind the actuality of the things symbolized, and whatever truth he sees or thinks he sees he develops himself, hoping that his concepts somehow accord with a universality that is probably forever beyond him. The difficulty that often arises, however, is that there are times in which the symbol becomes more important than the thing symbolized, as, for example, when the aesthetic nature of mathematical purity is obscured by an emphasis on the symbols of that purity, or when the singers, costumes, scenery, settings, resplendent theaters, and so forth of opera become more important than the meaning that should underlie them. All this is merely to suggest that all communication and all art, certainly including opera, is an attempt to balance symbol and thing symbolized. The attempt is successful when the communication is received and when the means used, however beautiful in itself, is subordinate to the impression conveyed. Such an observation may be fairly obvious, but much resistance to art and, particularly to opera—often not by any means totally unjustified—stems from a mistaken emphasis on form rather than content. It is often good and even essential to have an understanding of the form—this comes from experience and study—but it is better to feel what is beyond the form, and this requires more heart than mind.

There have been many ponderous tomes written about opera. Some describe in scholarly and excruciatingly serious detail the historical development of opera. Others present perceptive analyses of the complexities of Italian, German, French, Russian, or American opera. Others deal with the exhausting minutiae of individual operatic plots and settings and offer critical and explanatory expositions of them, while still others dissect musical structure and its relationship to dramatic action and to the nature and disposition of individual characters in particular operas. All these efforts are doubtless good, of great value and often very nearly definitive, and we will, therefore, in this book leave such erudite analyses to those better equipped and more inclined than we to handle them. We will be content merely to cast a slightly myopic and occasionally somewhat skeptical eye on a few scattered operas.

The choice of the operas that appear here, incidentally, we cannot justify in any reasonable way. Perhaps the selection resulted from the vagaries of our particular tastes or from chance motivation. Regardless, it should be emphasized that our choice should not be presumed to have any significance; it has merely resulted in a few tales from a few great operas. We were tempted, however, during the process of the selection to increase the volume, scope, and value of this book by listing and briefly describing, for the edification of the reader, all of the 28,000 or so operas that are in the possession of the Bibliothèque Nationale in Paris, and there are, indeed, at least that many scores reposing quietly there. But we decided to forbear, and in consequence, must humbly ask our readers' kind forgiveness.

Finally, although we are aware of the futility of undertaking to rationalize the essentially irrational, we probably should, nonetheless, acknowledge and at least make an attempt to explain both the title of this book and our use of sheep—lambs, ewes, and rams—in the illustrations that accompany the individual operas with which we have been concerned.

The first point to be made, then, is that Charles and Mary Lamb's *Tales from Shakespeare*—known as a handy shortcut to a great many readers who found themselves a bit diffident at the prospect of attacking Shakespeare "au naturel," as it were—suggested to us our title. But it suggested more than that, for what the original *Lambs' Tales* was trying to do for Shakespeare, we have tried in some sense to do for opera. Our purpose, as was that of the Lambs, was not solely to explain or to elucidate—the Lambs acknowledged the impossibility of doing that in any final sort of way for Shakespearean drama as we acknowledge it for opera—but as much or more to invite all to enter a world of immense and enriching aesthetic and sensuous experience. The Lambs aimed at an audience of children, particularly young gentlemen, of whom they requested with a quaintness happily reserved to a time somewhat less concerned with the equality of the sexes than our own may be, a "kind assistance . . . in explaining to their sisters such parts as are hardest for them to understand . . . carefully selecting what is proper for a young sister's ear." What we have to say and to show, however, is for all eyes and ears, and the invitation is—as it should probably always be—for any who will accept it.

But while our purpose may be akin to that of Charles and Mary Lamb, our means are certainly vastly different. To them we somehow owe our initial entanglements with the wooly brethren, but our expansion of that original involvement is, happily or not, solely ours. That there is often a truth that lies at the heart of absurdity is almost a fact of human existence or, at least, of our varying and flexible perceptions of existence, and it may be that we can see more of whatever is essentially true by looking at what may objectively not be true. Lewis Carroll knew this, as did the creator of the bustle and—probably—the composers of opera. The March Hare, the bustle, the romantic bellowings of an operatic diva of truly heroic proportions are absurd and meaningless to those who believe that reality is of only one shape. But to those who realize that truth is revealed in many forms, that rabbits or pigs or sheep or frogs or alligators being human may sometimes show us more than humans being human, the door to experience is always open. It is a door, in short, that is surely closed to those whose concept of reality always requires the objectively and drearily real.

On the other hand, perhaps the answer is much simpler. Perhaps, as the Chesire Cat once said to Alice, "We're all mad here. I'm mad. You're mad. You must be, or you wouldn't have come here."

At any rate, since we *are* here, and since you have *come* here, here for your pleasure are a few lambs' tales from a few great operas.

Lambs' Tales from Great Operas

PART ONE

The Eighteenth Century

Although there are a number of significant contributions to the canon of operatic works that are dated prior to the eighteenth century—those of Monteverdi, Pergolesi, Cavalli, Peri, and Purcell, for example, to note but a few—the repertory of regularly produced works of most modern opera houses begins with operas from the eighteenth century, those of Gluck and—most notably—of Mozart.

Modern opera had its real birth in the eighteenth century, and we include here as somewhat representative of this era Orfeo ed Euridice, *by Gluck, and* The Magic Flute, *by Mozart. Gluck was an artist of no mean proportions, but Mozart was a musical giant, a transcendent figure in all musical forms at whose feet nearly all composers of any century sit in awed wonderment. Despite the fact that Mozart lived only some thirty-five years, his musical output was prodigious, and it included no less than eight operas, of which we have here, arbitrarily, chosen just one.*

ORFEO ED EURIDICE

An Opera in Three Acts
by Christoph Willibald von Gluck (1714–1787)
with Libretto by Ranieri Calzabigi

Based on the Greek legend of Orfeo and Euridice; first per-
formed at the Hofburg Theater, Vienna, on October 5, 1762.
The setting is in the Greece of antiquity and in the Underworld.
The original language was Italian.

Characters

Orfeo .... *Contralto*
Euridice .... *Soprano*
Amor—*the God of Love* .... *Soprano*
A Happy Shade .... *Soprano*
Nymphs, shepherds and shepherdesses,
Furies and Demons, Heroes and Heroines
in the Underworld, attendants, etc.

Orfeo ed Euridice

Although opera, in its broadest terms, did not originate with Gluck—he was preceded by operatic composers such as Monteverdi and Cavalli—he is probably the earliest composer whose operas are more or less regularly performed by modern repertory companies. Opera had in the seventeenth century become primarily a vehicle for singers to use in exhibiting their voices. It was Gluck who made the leap—radical in that day—to a genuine operatic form that combined the power of a vibrant story, the strength of a developed musical form, and the talents of both vocal and instrumental performers into a unified and balanced whole. And *Orfeo ed Euridice* is probably the oldest example of what we would today consider a genuine and fully realized operatic creation.

And it is without question magnificent. Orfeo, who is a Greek minstrel, is able, through the sheer beauty of his music, so to charm and soften the hearts of the keepers of the underworld—the Furies, the three-headed dog, Cerberus, the fierce Eumenides—that he is allowed to enter and attempt to lead back to the real world his lost love, Euridice. If his music can successfully move the hearts of the apparently heartless, is it not evident that such an accomplishment is intended to parallel the essential raison d'etre of all art?

The gods, themselves moved by Orfeo's anguish at the loss of Euridice, have given him the opportunity to attempt to redeem her, but there is—as always—a condition imposed. On his journey from Hades back to his world, he cannot look at Euridice nor explain why he must avert his gaze: if he does, she will die, this time, the gods guarantee, irretrievably. Euridice, whose love for Orfeo is not, apparently, of sufficient

"... to Euridice, all unknowing, the passion of the moment is foremost ..."

stature to enable her to trust him completely nor whose desire for his attention is within manageable dimensions, so entreats, cajoles, and threatens him with a refusal to follow that Orfeo finally, in agony and in defiance of the gods, turns and passionately embraces her. Instantly she dies, and Orfeo, who believes what the deities have told him, prepares to kill himself rather than endure separation from Euridice once more. But his suicidal hand is stayed by Amor, the god of love, and the gods, in admiration for his steadfastness, loyalty, and courage, proclaim that Euridice will be returned to him anyway.

Now, there is no question that for some tastes there is a satisfaction to be derived from the happy resolution of a situation that is supposed to be by definition irresolvable. But to other tastes, there is something as unsatisfying and unsettling in such a denouement as there is in that of the biblical story of Jacob and his son, Isaac, in which Jacob's knife is at the ultimate moment kept from Isaac's throat by an angel who announces that God was only testing Jacob's faith and that his son is not to be sacrificed after all. Jacob is properly thankful, and it never occurs to him to question the essential character of a God who would put him to such a cruel test, although to more modern sensibilities a good deal of rage might not be an unexpected reaction. Analogously, when Orfeo breaks the rules of the game and the expected result is almost capriciously changed, the reaction of a Western man who is deeply convinced of the significance of his role as a responsible human being in the entire scheme of things is rather predictably a bit of outrage. But this is probably a minor point; more important is the sheer moving beauty of Gluck's music and the immensely effective wholeness of the entire work.

In the illustration we see Orfeo, a tear glimmering in his eye, leading his beloved Euridice from the underworld. He has been forbidden to look upon her, but to Euridice, all unknowing, the passion of the moment is foremost as she plies her irresistible blandishments upon her lover.

[6   ]

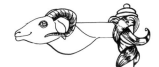

THE MAGIC FLUTE
(Die Zauberflöte)

An Opera in Two Acts
by Wolfgang Amadeus Mozart (1756–1791)
with Libretto by Emanuel Schikaneder
and Johann Georg Metzler (Giesecke)

Based on the Oriental story, *Lulu,* by Liebeskind; first performed at Theater an der Wien, Vienna, on September 30, 1791. The setting is in and around the Temple of Isis in ancient Egypt, at about the time of Rameses I. The original language was German.

Characters

Tamino—*an Egyptian Prince* .... *Tenor*
Three Ladies—*attendants of the*   *Two Sopranos and*
         Queen of Night .... *Mezzo-Soprano*
Papageno—*a birdcatcher* .... *Baritone*
The Queen of Night .... *Soprano*
Monostatos—*a moor, slave to Sarastro* .... *Tenor*
Pamina—*daughter of the Queen of Night* .... *Soprano*
Three Genii .... *Soprano, Mezzo-Soprano, Contralto*
The Orator .... *Bass*
Sarastro—*High Priest of Isis and Osiris* .... *Bass*
Two Priests .... *Tenor and Bass*
Papagena .... *Soprano*
Two Men in Armor .... *Tenor and Bass*
    Slaves, priests, attendants, people, etc.

The Magic Flute
(Die Zauberflöte)

There can be little doubt that as long as opera survives, *Die Zauberflöte* will continue to be performed and enjoyed and loved. The combination of Mozart's incomparable music with the delightful—if highly convoluted—story produces entertainment that has captivated audiences for nearly two hundred years.

The setting of the opera is somewhat indistinctly Egyptian, with an aura of temples and palaces and palm trees and sacred inner shrines, while the plot is something of a jumble that includes sorcery, a wicked queen, instant love, a treacherous Moor, and symbolic parallels—of considerably more interest in Mozart's time than in ours—to Freemasonry, the Empress Maria Theresa, the Austrian people, and God (or Mozart) only knows what else.

Basically the story revolves around the efforts of Prince Tamino, assisted by the fairly simple-minded birdcatcher, Papageno, to prove himself worthy of the beautiful Pamina, daughter of the Queen of Night, who is being held captive by the sorcerer, Sarastro. It turns out, finally, that Sarastro is really a fine and straightforward—if a bit serious—fellow, while the Queen of Night and her entourage are the possessors of essentially flawed characters. Ostensibly, it is Tamino and Pamina, inflamed by passion even though they don't know each other, who supply the major romantic thrust of the story, but it is Papageno, by turns happy-go-lucky, frightened, deceptive, and poignantly in search of a paramour—one turns up for him in the form of Papagena—who captures our main interest. Tamino possesses the magic flute,

". . . handsome Prince Tamino receiving the magic flute . . ."

whose golden notes turn the hardest hearts from belligerence to love, but Papageno has a set of chimes, which he uses with telling effect, that have the power to render all opposition impotent. Everything, naturally, becomes resolved in the most satisfactory manner by the time the opera is finished—the Queen of Night and her retinue go screaming down to hell, for example—but the most pleasing resolution comes for the audience through the sheer joy of experiencing the enchanting opera as a whole.

It may be that an ultra-sensitive social consciousness might look a bit askance at the juxtaposition of a noble love—that of the patrician and courageous Prince Tamino and the Princess Pamina—and the unabashedly plebeian and comic counterpart between the simple and faint-hearted Papageno and his Papagena, but who cares, really, about such delicacy of sentiment in the context of great art.

In the drawing on the preceding page, we see the handsome Prince Tamino receiving the magic flute from one of the attendants of the Queen of Night. Papageno, the bird-catcher, stands rather disconsolately behind Prince Tamino, a trifle miffed that he has not been given anything comparable. It is a bit later that, terrified, he receives the chimes from the three ladies as a protection for the coming ordeal that he is to share with Tamino as they set about freeing the captive Pamina.

PART TWO

The Nineteenth Century

If the eighteenth century saw the emergence of a truly oper-atic form, the nineteenth century was the time of its flowering and its development into an elaborate and highly variegated ar-tistic expression. Opera spread beyond the parochial limitations of its adolescence, and it began to make full use of the immense resources at its disposal. It reflected the great artistic movements of the times, and it gave the world an enduring legacy of imper-ishable value.

From this period we have chosen eleven operas, again rather arbitrarily, as being at least somewhat representative of this vast outpouring of esthetic creativity. It must be remem-bered, however, that these operas, despite their intrinsic values, represent only a tiny glimpse into this enormous world. (Verdi, alone, for example, produced at least sixteen operas, and he was only one—a gigantic one, to be sure, but still only one—of liter-ally scores of operatic composers.) But a glimpse, however lim-ited, may lead to curiosity, to exploration, and eventually to that broader view of art that has the capacity of imparting such truly remarkable and splendid rewards.

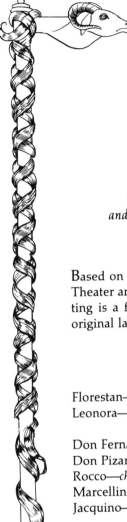
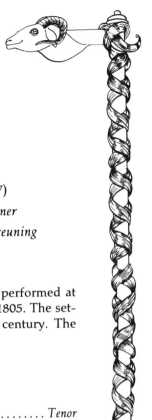

FIDELIO

An Opera in Two Acts
by Ludwig van Beethoven (1770–1827)
with original Libretto by Josef Sonnleithner
and subsequent revisions by Stephan von Breuning
and Georg Friedrich Treitschke

Based on a drama by Jean Nicolas Bouilly; first performed at Theater an der Wien, Vienna, on November 20, 1805. The setting is a fortress near Seville in the eighteenth century. The original language was German.

Characters

Florestan—*a Spanish nobleman* .... *Tenor*
Leonora—*Florestan's wife, disguised in male attire*
          as Fidelio .... *Soprano*
Don Fernando—*Prime Minister of Spain* .... *Bass*
Don Pizarro—*governor of the prison fortress of Seville* .... *Bass*
Rocco—*chief jailer at the fortress* .... *Bass*
Marcellina—*daughter of Rocco* .... *Soprano*
Jacquino—*assistant to Rocco* .... *Tenor*
       Soldiers, prisoners, townspeople

Fidelio

It is probably not really remarkable that *Fidelio* is Beethoven's sole opera, for the master, although he produced a number of works requiring the human voice, was certainly not an operatic composer such as, for example, Donizetti, Verdi, Puccini, Rossini, or Wagner. This does not mean that *Fidelio* is in any sense an inferior work—it is quite the opposite, actually—or that Beethoven did not give to it the attention or dedication that it deserved—he devoted a vast amount of time to its composition and to a number of meticulous revisions. But it was his only venture into the operatic genre, and even were it not for the opera's intrinsic merits, which are many, it would be interesting for that reason alone.

The story and the libretto appealed to Beethoven's profoundly idealistic soul. He probably saw in it indications of human characteristics that were of great importance to him—the transcendent power of feeling and the nobility of the spirit—and there seems little question that his mind and heart were deeply bound up in the work. Basically, the plot has to do with the efforts of Leonore, the wife of Florestan, to effect her husband's release from the prison where he has been incarcerated by Don Pizarro, the governor of the prison, for base and unworthy reasons and where he is in imminent danger of death. In order to further this laudable enterprise, Leonore resorts to the ruse of diguising herself as a young man, calling herself Fidelio, so that she can secure employment as an assistant to the chief jailer, Rocco, and, presumably, find an opportunity to save Florestan. Her plans are complicated somewhat by the fact that Rocco's daughter, Marcellina, falls in love with the handsome youth whom she knows as Fidelio, rejecting in the process, at least temporarily, her former suitor, Jacquino. Don Pizarro, having fomented the rumor that Florestan is dead, decides—when he

". . . Leonore and Florestan . . . as they embrace and sing a rap-
turous duet."

learns that the King's Minister, Don Fernando, is contemplating a visit to investigate charges that some inmates have been unjustly imprisoned—that he must actually kill him and dispose of the body. Rocco has sturdily refused to commit the nefarious deed, and Pizarro resolves that he must carry it out himself.

On orders from Pizarro, Leonore-Fidelio goes to the dungeon with Rocco to help prepare a secret grave for Florestan, and when Don Pizarro enters with a view to dispatching Florestan forthwith, she throws herself between them, menaces Don Pizarro with a pistol she has brought with her, and declares in ringing tones that if he is to kill Florestan, he must first kill his wife.

Pizarro had taken the precaution, earlier, of posting a sentry on the prison battlements to warn him of the approach of the Prime Minister, and at the climactic moment in the dungeon the clarion call of the sentry's trumpet is heard, notes which Beethoven incorporated in the Leonore Overture No. 3, usually performed as a prelude to the scene that follows and concludes the opera. It is an excruciatingly dramatic moment, both musically and literarily, and it unmistakably signals the triumph of justice and right over evil and treachery. All is eventually resolved in the next scene, with Pizarro being unmasked as the scoundrel he is, Florestan being recognized and liberated by his friend, the Minister, and the loving and loyal Leonore being finally reunited with her ecstatically appreciative husband.

In the illustration, we see the tender and moving reunion of Leonore and Florestan in the latter's prison cell, as they embrace and sing a rapturous duet prior to emerging into the town square, where all is finally set right by the good Don Fernando.

What happens to Marcellina, left, somehow, in a fundamental lurch, remains unresolved.

THE BARBER OF SEVILLE

An Opera in Two Acts
by Gioachino Antonio Rossini (1792–1868)
with Libretto by Cesare Sterbini

Based on the comedy, *Le Barbiere de Séville*, by the French dramatist, Beaumarchais; first performed at the Teatro Argentino, Rome, on February 5, 1816. The setting is the city of Seville, Spain, in the seventeenth century. The original language was Italian.

Characters

Count Almaviva .... *Tenor*
Doctor Bartolo .... *Bass*
Don Basilio—*a music teacher* .... *Bass*
Figaro—*a barber* .... *Baritone*
Fiorello—*a servant of Count Almaviva* .... *Bass*
Ambrogio—*a servant of Doctor Bartolo* .... *Bass*
Rosina—*ward of Doctor Bartolo* .... *Mezzo-Soprano*
Berta—*housemaid of Doctor Bartolo; governess of Rosina* .. *Soprano*
A magistrate, a notary, a constable,
musicians, and soldiers

The Barber of Seville

One of the best known and most popular of all comic operas, Rossini's *Il Barbiere di Siviglia*, is an operatic rendition of the first part of a dramatic triology by the eighteenth-century French playwright, Beaumarchais. It also parallels the general line of an earlier opera composed by Giovanni Paisiello, a contemporary of Rossini's, and its composition followed Mozart's famous *The Marriage of Figaro*—a rendering of the second part of the *Barbiere* trilogy—by some thirty years.

Figaro *is* the barber of Seville, and he is also the town busy-body and gossip, the jack-of-all-trades and the clever, if somewhat unrefined, schemer and finagler. His values do not rise too much above gold and his vast estimation of his own importance, but life is, nonetheless, a huge amount of fun for him, and he enjoys intrigues, girls and young widows, and his guitar with a totally unrestrained joie de vivre.

The plot of *The Barber of Seville* revolves around the delightful attempts of Figaro to arrange the marriage of the Count Almaviva, a Spanish Grandee, to the beautiful Rosina, the ward of one Dr. Bartolo, a crotchety old wretch who wants, himself, to marry Rosina. Confusion reigns, naturally, during much of the opera, through misunderstandings, secret letters, mistaken identities, and so forth, but in the end Figaro's machinations prevail, the happy pair are wed, and Dr. Bartolo ruefully accepts the end result of the somewhat muddled but nonetheless triumphant course of true love.

The music of the opera, the delightful arias, and the convolutions of the plot are splendid entertainment, but it is without doubt Figaro who, although no more strictly central

". . . the best barber in all Christendom . . ."

to the plot than Puck or Sancho Panza, is our chief delight.

In the drawing on the preceding page, Figaro is shown in his basic vocation, that of the barber, but there is little question that although he considers himself to be the best barber in all Christendom, his other less formal occupations are the sources of the principal pleasures in his life.

LUCIA DI LAMMERMOOR

An Opera in Three Acts
by Gaetano Donizetti (1797–1848)
with Libretto by Salvatore Cammarano

Based on the novel, *The Bride of Lammermoor*, by Sir Walter Scott; first performed at Teatro San Carlo, Naples, on September 26, 1835. The setting is Scotland, at the beginning of the eighteenth century.

Characters

Lord Enrico Ashton, *of Lammermoor—a Scotch*
　　　　　　　　　nobleman .... *Baritone*
Lucia Ashton—*Lord Enrico's sister* .... *Soprano*
Sir Edgardo, *of Ravenswood—last of his family* .... *Tenor*
Lord Arturo Bucklaw—*a nobleman of means and*
　　　　　　　　　influence .... *Tenor*
Raimondo—*a chaplain at Lammermoor and Lucia's tutor* .... Bass
Alisa—*Lucia's companion* .... *Mezzo-Soprano*
Normanno—*Lord Enrico Ashton's captain of the guard* ..... *Tenor*
　　　　Family, relatives, retainers, pages, soldiers
　　　　and servants of the House of Lammermoor

Lucia di Lammermoor

It is remarkable how faithless apparently profound faith often turns out to be. Perhaps it is the very purity of the nearly perfect that renders it so vulnerable and fragile. As a contrast, perhaps it is the redeemable sinner, the slightly flawed sceptic, the impure lover who has the greatest resistance to assaults and the greatest possibility of survival in the face of adversity.

Be that as it may, the list of romantic heroes and heroines who, despite—or, possibly, because of—the depth and purity of their loves, have shown a deplorable and astounding inability to resist challenge or the invidious suggestions that their lovers are unfaithful, is a nearly endless one.

A case in point is found in Donizetti's great opera, *Lucia di Lammermoor.* Much like the Montagues and Capulets of *Romeo and Juliet,* the noble Scottish families of Lammermoor and Ravenswood have been mortal enemies of long standing. Naturally, Lucia, who is a Lammermoor, and Edgardo, the last survivor of the Ravenswood clan, are passionately in love. And equally naturally, when Lucia's brother, Enrico, suggests to his sister—for nefarious reasons of his own—that she should marry Arturo, a nobleman whose financial assistance Enrico direly needs, and when he produces a forged letter indicating that Edgardo has been faithless, Lucia's faith crumbles. She also begins to die, although the process takes a while.

Eventually Edgardo shows up. He is presented with the marriage contract that Lucia, in a nearly irrational state, has signed with Arturo, and he instantly assumes that Lucia has

"The lovers discuss their unhappy position at some length . . ."

been unfaithful to him, and he denounces her in ringing and bitter tones.

Well, who, really, can blame either of them, although one may be permitted to wonder just what they meant when, at the end of Act I of the opera, they pledged their complete faith and devotion to each other. It is this scene, incidentally, that is depicted on the preceding page. Lucia and Edgardo have met in a park, near a fountain that, as Lucia sings in a dramatic and foreshadowing aria, is the legendary site of a previous tragic love tryst. The lovers discuss their unhappy position at some length and with considerable passion, and it is at this point that, with an exchange of rings, they express their heartfelt but ephemeral pledges.

Lucia must eventually, of course, die, and she does in Act III, mad with disappointment and with the agony of her unfulfilled love for Edgardo. She has managed, a bit earlier, to stab her unwelcome husband to death, which takes care of him and demonstrates clearly to everyone that she is regrettably but unquestionably deranged. Edgardo, too, unable to bear the pain, stabs himself at the end of the opera, and only Enrico—among the main characters—is left to live with and reflect upon the tragedy of which he, basically, was the cause. Presumably, Lucia and Edgardo—who really *did* mean to be everlastingly devoted to each other—consummate their love in Heaven, where faith and fervor can exist in utter peace, without the disturbance of unwelcome tests.

LA TRAVIATA

An Opera in Three Acts
by Giuseppe Verdi (1813–1901)
with Libretto by Francesco Maria Piave

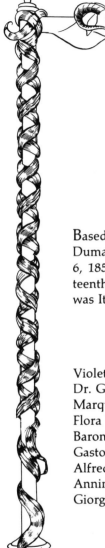

Based on the drama, *La Dame aux Camélias*, by Alexandre Dumas; first performed at Teatro la Fenice, Venice, on March 6, 1853. The setting is in and about Paris, in the early eighteenth century, the time of Louis XIV. The original language was Italian.

Characters

Violetta Valery—*a courtesan* . . . . *Soprano*
Dr. Grenvil—*physician to Violetta* . . . . *Bass*
Marquis d'Obigny—*a nobleman* . . . . *Bass*
Flora Bervoix—*a friend of Violetta* . . . . *Mezzo-Soprano*
Baron Douphol—*a rival of Alfredo* . . . . *Baritone*
Gastone—*Viscount of Letorieres* . . . . *Tenor*
Alfredo Germont—*lover of Violetta* . . . . *Tenor*
Annina—*maid and confidante of Violetta* . . . . *Mezzo-Soprano*
Giorgio Germont—*father of Alfredo* . . . . *Baritone*
Salon guests, masqueraders, dancers,
servants, picadors, gypsies

La Traviata

St. Augustine, back in the fifth century, pondered over the puzzling paradox of why people derived a high degree of pleasure from seeing occurrences on the stage that they would be exceedingly loath to see happen to themselves. He considered this to be a perversity of human nature, ungodly and an experience to be avoided. Be that as it may, there is little doubt that a tale involving a straightforward love affair that progresses painlessly and without complications would not be much of a story, as happy as such a situation might be in real life.

Opera is, of course, no exception to this general dramatic rule, and *La Traviata* is replete with the tragic and fatal consequences that attend a true but somewhat impossible love. Violetta, a Parisian courtesan and a devout believer in the philosophy that pleasure is the supreme goal of existence, is converted from her exclusively hedonistic approach to life by the true love of Alfredo, a young man from a respected provincial family. It would appear that both have found happiness through love and the realization of certain basic truths about life, but Alfredo's father shows up punctually and quickly ruins everything by noting that Violetta's lurid background and her current relationship with Alfredo are doing him and his family no good at all, particularly with regard to his daughter's impending wedding. He tells Violetta that she must, for the greater good of everyone else concerned, give up Alfredo, a suggestion that understandably throws her into a turmoil, although she accepts—fairly readily, it must be said—the necessity for such a sacrifice.

". . . Alfredo . . . smitten and undone at the sight of Violetta . . ."

To the approval, presumably, of the audience, agony now prevails. Violetta pretends to love another; Alfredo, with the essentially limited vision required in order for the plot to spin itself out, predictably misunderstands; and everything moves towards a satisfactory conclusion when Alfredo's father, inspired by his tardy realization of the depth of Alfredo's and Violetta's feelings for each other, confesses his part in the turn of events. Belatedly he assures them both of his blessing, but Violetta is at this point too far gone, and despite her struggles with a vaguely undefined illness, she finally expires, to the great chagrin of those around her and the great satisfaction of the opera audience, who have known all along that it all had to turn out this way.

It is a sad and tragic opera, but there are a good many moments of gaiety and festivity, as would befit the sophisticated life of a Parisian courtesan of the first order. In the scene depicted on the preceding page, a happy scene of a fashionable soirée thrown by Violetta, we see Alfredo on the right, smitten and undone at the sight of Violetta as she sings her famous "champagne aria" and simultaneously gives him the eye. Thus begins the course of true but misbegotten love. Poor Alfredo! Poor Violetta!

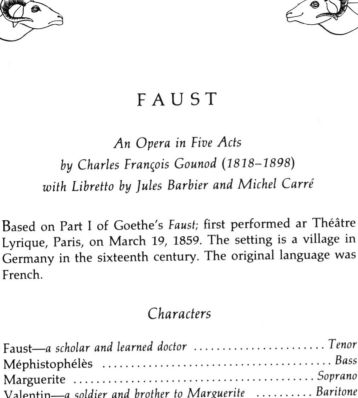

FAUST

An Opera in Five Acts
by Charles François Gounod (1818–1898)
with Libretto by Jules Barbier and Michel Carré

Based on Part I of Goethe's *Faust;* first performed ar Théâtre Lyrique, Paris, on March 19, 1859. The setting is a village in Germany in the sixteenth century. The original language was French.

Characters

Faust—*a scholar and learned doctor* .... *Tenor*
Méphistophélès .... *Bass*
Marguerite .... *Soprano*
Valentin—*a soldier and brother to Marguerite* .... *Baritone*
Siebel—*a village youth in love with Marguerite* ... *Mezzo-Soprano*
Wagner—*a young student* .... *Baritone*
Martha Schwerlein—*a neighbor and friend of*
         Marguerite .... *Mezzo-Soprano*
Soldiers, students, villagers, angels, demons,
dancers, Cleopatra, Helen of Troy, and others

Faust

The legend of Faust is so pervasive in our Western culture that it has become indelibly associated with the West's deepest characteristics and most profound manifestations. The story has formed the basis for countless artistic expressions, from painting to drama to poetry to music, and not the least of these is the opera by Gounod.

Perhaps the most developed, monumental, and, indeed, nearly definitive of all works on the Faustian theme is that of Goethe, and it is a small part of this version—with certain notable variations—that forms the basis for Gounod's opera. In the most general terms, the legend involves the pact made by Faust—the scholar, the frustrated searcher for truth and meaning—with Méphistophélès—the emissary of Satan, the embodiment of evil—in which, in exchange for the gratification of his earthly desires, Faust cedes his soul to the powers of darkness. In most versions, although Faust does achieve certain desires that are somewhat less than noble, he usually emerges clearly as a sincere searcher for truth, beauty, and understanding. That he uses the devil as a means to further his quest obviously touches on the age-old question of ends and means, and there is little doubt that his eventual doom comes as the result of the thoroughly illegitimate means he uses.

Of an importance nearly equivalent to that of Faust and of Méphistophélès, Marguerite appears in the Faustian legend as the initial paramour whom Faust desires. His relation with her is that part of the entire saga upon which Gounod based his opera.

"... Méphistophélès—

the emissary of Satan, the embodiment of evil ..."

The opera, like nearly all versions of the legend, opens with Faust seated at his desk and engaged in a scholarly but futile study of life and the world that culminates in his desperate invocation of Méphistophélès. With his satanic powers, Méphistophélès induces Faust to sign the fatal pact, and in return Faust, rendered youthful, is enabled to court the lovely Marguerite. With the help of Méphistophélès, against whom the only effective power is a pure Christian faith, Faust consummates an illicit love with Marguerite and manages to kill her brother in the bargain. Marguerite, mad with remorse and guilt, slays her child, for which she is condemned to death, but in the final scene, in her prison cell, she achieves her redemption through her total reliance on heavenly powers, while Faust is dragged away to his eternal damnation by Méphistophélès.

Such a summary does little justice to the powerful music of the opera or to the pervasive and primeval struggle between the gloating Méphistophélès and the unfortunate sinners with whom he comes into contact. Suffice it to say that the essential message has at its heart the concept that man, whose role on Earth is necessarily limited by his human weaknesses, is capable of achieving salvation not through his own efforts or—certainly—through those of the forces of the underworld, but only through faith in the power and beneficence of the Almighty.

In the illustration we see Méphistophélès, resplendent in his accouterments and balefully exhibiting the powers of evil and darkness of which he is master.

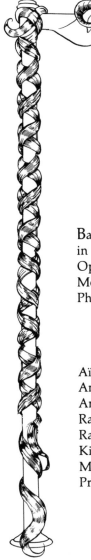
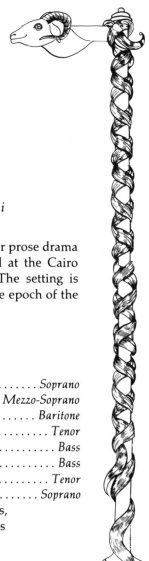

AÏDA

An Opera in Four Acts
by Giuseppe Verdi (1813–1901)
with Libretto by Antonio Ghislanzoni

Based on a plot sketch by Mariette Bey and a later prose drama in French by Camille du Locle; first performed at the Cairo Opera House, Cairo, on December 24, 1871. The setting is Memphis and Thebes in ancient Egypt during the epoch of the Pharaohs. The original language was Italian.

Characters

Aïda—*an Ethiopian girl, slave to Amneris* .... *Soprano*
Amneris—*daughter of the King of Egypt* .... *Mezzo-Soprano*
Amonasro—*King of Ethiopia, father of Aïda* .... *Baritone*
Radames—*Captain of the Egyptian guard* .... *Tenor*
Ramphis—*a High Priest of Isis* .... *Bass*
King of Egypt—*father of Amneris* .... *Bass*
Messenger .... *Tenor*
Priestess .... *Soprano*
Priests, priestesses, Ethiopian slaves,
guards, dancers, soldiers, Egyptians

Aïda

Amid the splendor and pageantry of ancient Egypt in the days of the Pharaohs is spun the tale of Aïda, the hapless Ethiopian princess, who has been enslaved by the Egyptians. The love she shares with the equally hapless Radames, the Egyptian military conqueror of the Ethiopians, is doomed not so much by the workings of a kind of inexorable destiny as it is by the workings of the Pharaoh's daughter, Amneris, who—herself hopelessly in love with the unresponsive Radames—completes the fatal triangle.

Radames is in the unenviable position of being simultaneously the hero of the Egyptian victory over the Ethiopians—fêted by a grateful nation and rewarded by the Pharaoh—and also in love with the daughter of the King he has newly vanquished, by definition an enemy of the people. Even during his triumphant return—in the scene that contains the stirring "Triumphal March from *Aïda*," one of the best known of all operatic passages—he is torn by the insoluble nature of his dual loyalties. But his dilemma is matched by that of Aïda, for she, steadfastly loyal to the country of her birth and to her father, loves the greatest enemy of her homeland. Naturally, their relationship must be a clandestine one, but it is Amneris who ferrets out Aïda's secret and who throughout the opera seethes in the throes of her jealousy and her unrequited love.

Aïda, goaded by her father, becomes an unwilling participant in a scheme to trick Radames into revealing a crucial military secret, and at the moment that he unwittingly but treasonously reveals the secret, Amneris and the high priest

"*. . . Amneris, convulsed by the agony of Radames' fate . . .*"

rush from the nearby temple to denounce him. Radames is condemned to death, disdaining the opportunities proffered to him by Amneris to save himself in return for renouncing Aïda. He accepts the sentence of being entombed alive beneath the Temple of Vulcan, preferring death to a life without honor and, above all, without Aïda.

The final scene of the opera takes place in a kind of double setting. The upper part is the temple, while below is the tomb in which Radames has been placed. As he laments the loss of Aïda, he suddenly sees her in the tomb, where she has secreted herself to share death with him as she could not share life. It is this scene which is shown in the illustration on the preceding page, where we see Aïda and Radames singing their love for each other. Amneris, convulsed by the agony of Radames' fate, remains outside the tomb, condemned to live with her guilt and with the anguish of her bereavement.

BORIS GODUNOV

An Opera in a Prologue and Four Acts
by Modest Petrovich Mussorgsky (1839–1881)
with Libretto by the Composer

Following a drama of the same title by Pushkin, and Karamzin's *History of the Russian Empire,* and based on an actual episode in Russian history; subject to a multitude of revisions over a number of years by both Mussorgsky and Rimsky-Korsakov; first performed in its entirety probably about 1874. The setting is Russia and Poland between 1598 and 1605. The original language was Russian.

Characters

Boris Godunov .... *Baritone*
Feodor—*son of Boris* .... *Mezzo-Soprano*
Xenia—*daughter of Boris* .... *Soprano*
An Old Nurse .... *Contralto*
Prince Shuisky—*a court adviser to Boris* .... *Tenor*
Andrei Shchelkalov—*clerk of the Duma* .... *Baritone*
Pimen—*a monk and a chronicler of history* .... *Bass*
Grigory—*a novice, later, Dmitri, Pretender to the throne* .... *Tenor*
Marina Mnishek—*a Polish Princess and landowner's*
                daughter .... *Soprano*
Rangoni—*a Jesuit Priest in disguise* .... *Bass*
Varlaam *and* Missail—*vagabond mendicant*
                friars .... *Bass and Tenor*
The Hostess of the Inn .... *Mezzo-Soprano*
Nikitin—*a constable* .... *Bass*
The Idiot .... *Tenor*
Lavitsky *and* Chernikovsky—*Jesuit Priests* .... *Basses*
    Russian people, soldiers, guards, pilgrims,
       children, court attendants

Boris Godunov

It would be an overstatement, of course, to say that *all* Russian literature revolves around either the revolutionary struggles of oppressed masses or the psychological struggles of oppressed minds, but certainly a good portion of it does, and the opera *Boris Godunov*, based on a Pushkin drama—itself based on a true incident in Russian history—is no exception to the general rule. Replete with revolutionary zeal, fiery ambition for power, political and personal intrigue, and the agonies of guilty conscience, *Boris Godunov* is a panoramic Russian display of the tangled relations of royalty, aristocracy, clergy, and the peasantry.

Boris, like Macbeth, is tortured by memories that he cannot dismiss, in this case those involved with his role in the murder of Dmitri, the younger brother of Czar Feodor, son of Ivan the Terrible and legal successor to Feodor's throne. Although Dmitri is dead, there is a kind of mystical aura that surrounds his spirit, and much like Macbeth, who is nearly undone by his vision of the ghost of the murdered Banquo, Boris, who had become Czar upon Feodor's death, cannot rid himself of the shadow of Dmitri that haunts him. In addition, a young monk, Grigory, has taken upon himself the role of Dmitri, and—with the help of the politically ambitious daughter of a Polish landowner, Marina, whom he loves, and that of Rangoni, an oily Jesuit who thirsts for power—has launched an attack on Boris based on his claim that he really is Dmitri.

The opera is filled with passion, suffering, avaricious desire, and insurrectionary fervor, and Mussorgsky's music is

"... Boris, on the throne

        which has become his through his treachery ..."

appropriately moving and grand. Boris, again like Macbeth, is a towering figure, and his role in the opera—encompassing moments of rage, tenderness, and deep human emotion and culminating in a dreadful mental anguish when he is at death's door—requires a singer of exceptional power. The very grandeur and scale of the opera have firmly established it as one of the finest products of the Russian school.

The scene depicted on the preceding page is of Boris, on the throne which has become his through his treachery. He is Russian, but the legacy of his ruthless Tartar forebears is clearly evident in him.

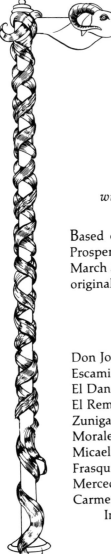
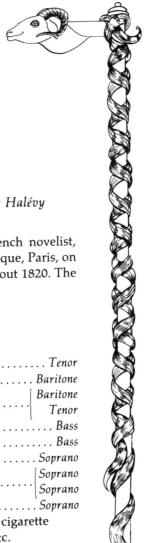

CARMEN

An Opera in Four Acts
by Georges Bizet (1838–1875)
with Libretto by Henri Meilhac and Ludovic Halévy

Based on a story of the same name by the French novelist, Prosper Mérimée; first performed at Opera-Comique, Paris, on March 3, 1875. The setting is Seville, Spain, in about 1820. The original language was French.

Characters

Don José—*a corporal of dragoons* .... Tenor
Escamillo—*a toreador* .... Baritone
El Dancairo ⎫ *smugglers* .... ⎰ Baritone
El Remendado ⎭ .... ⎱ Tenor
Zuniga—*a captain of dragoons* .... Bass
Morales—*an officer* .... Bass
Micaela—*a peasant girl* .... Soprano
Frasquita ⎫ *gypsy friends of Carmen* .... ⎰ Soprano
Mercedes ⎭ .... ⎱ Soprano
Carmen—*a gypsy and cigarette girl* .... Soprano
Innkeeper, guide, officers, dragoons, boys, cigarette
girls, gypsies, smugglers, dancers, etc.

Carmen

Carmen, one of the most beloved and enduring of all grand operas, has as its theme the familiar problem of ill-fated love and the faithlessness of imperfect humans. But it has touches of much more, for Carmen, herself, is the quintessential love object, the epitome of the passionate, the ultimate personification of ardent untamed spirit. And therein lies her inexorable tragedy, for her doom—pervasively intimated throughout the opera in repeated musical and literary suggestions—stems from the poignant reiteration of the fact that a bitter fate awaits the immoderate. This does not mean that only the moderate survive, for they often find their own unspectacular dooms in their own ways, but it does suggest that it is Carmen's own free and fiery nature that eventually consumes her. Throughout the opera it is clear that Carmen is aware of this, and, indeed, it is with a fatalistic sense of her own impending death—"Free was I born! Free will I die!" she sings in the final scene—that she steadfastly fulfills her nature.

But she would have it no other way. With Spanish gypsy blood coursing through her veins, she is the seductress who lives only through the intense, though fickle, exercise of her emotions. Without a flicker of remorse, she first lures Don José, a corporal of dragoons, into falling violently in love with her and then spurns him heartlessly when she spies a new conquest, Escamillo, the toreador, who, incidentally, knows perfectly well that—as he sings in Act III—"Carmen's love does not last." Don José has given up everything for Carmen—the love of the innocent and charming peasant girl,

"... sufficient to inflame the most listless of hearts ..."

Micaela, the responsibilities of his military duties, his very honor—and when he finally realizes that Carmen can no longer be his, in the jealous and nearly demented height of his passion, he plunges his poignard into her heart, even though it is only a moment later that he throws himself near her body and cries the last words of the opera, "Oh Carmen! My adored Carmen!"

Bizet's music and the dramatic Spanish setting of the opera are in complete harmony with the theme. The aura of the bull ring, the seductive flirtations of girls and soldiers, the constant and dangerous sparring between authority and outlaw are all much in evidence, and it is the hot sun of Seville that shines over all.

In this scene, from the first Act of the opera, we see Carmen, with her castanets and in her Spanish finery, performing a dance which is sufficient, persumably, to inflame the most listless of hearts.

DER RING DER NIBELUNGEN

A Cycle of Operatic Stage-Festival Plays Consisting of
Four Distinct but Dramatically and Musically Related Parts
by Richard Wagner (1813–1883)
with Libretto by the Composer

Based on Germanic, Icelandic, and Scandinavian Sagas, especially the Nibelungen Saga; first performed in its entirety in August 1876, at Bayreuth, Germany. The setting is the Germany of antiquity, and specifically includes the bed of the River Rhine, mountains, and other wild regions near the Rhine, the subterranean caverns of Nibelheim, and other desolate and untamed locales. The original language was German.

Characters

I. DAS RHEINGOLD
(The Rheingold)

Woglinde	....	*Soprano*
Wellgunde *Rhinemaidens*	....	*Soprano*
Flosshilde	....	*Mezzo-Soprano*
Alberich—*King of the Nibelungs*	....	Bass
Fricka—*wife of Wotan*	....	*Mezzo-Soprano*
Wotan—*King of the Gods*	....	Bass-Baritone
Freia—*sister of Fricka, Goddess of Youth and Beauty*	.....	*Soprano*
Fasolt		Bass
Fafner *giants*	....	Bass
Froh		*Tenor*
Donner—*the thunder God* *brothers of Freia*	....	*Baritone*
Loge—*the fire God*	....	*Tenor*
Mime—*brother of Alberich*	....	*Tenor*
Erda—*the earth Goddess*	....	*Mezzo-Soprano*

II. DIE WALKÜRE
(The Valkyr)

Siegmund ⎱ *Walsungs; mortal son and daughter of*	⎰ *Tenor*	
Sieglinde ⎰ *Wotan*	⎱ *Soprano*	

Hunding—*husband of Sieglinde* .... *Bass*
Wotan—*King of the Gods* .... *Bass-Baritone*
Brünnhilde—*daughter of Wotan and Erda,*
             eldest of the Valkyries .... *Soprano*
Fricka—*wife of Wotan* .... *Mezzo-Soprano*

Gerhilde
Ortlinde
Waltraute
Schwertleite   *Valkyries, other daughters of*   *Sopranos*
Helmwige   *Wotan and Erda* ....   *Mezzo-Sopranos*
Siegrune   *Contraltos*
Grimgerde
Rossweise

III. SIEGFRIED

Mime—*brother of Alberich* .... *Tenor*
Siegfried .... *Tenor*
Wotan—*(in disguise as the Wanderer)* .... *Bass-Baritone*
Alberich .... *Baritone*
Fafner—*(the dragon)* .... *Bass*
Forest Bird .... *Soprano*
Erda—*the earth goddess* .... *Contralto*
Brünnhilde .... *Soprano*

IV. DIE GÖTTERDÄMMERUNG
(The Twilight of the Gods)

First Norn   *Contralto*
Second Norn *daughters of Erda* .... *Mezzo-Soprano*
Third Norn   .... *Soprano*
Siegfried .... *Tenor*
Brünnhilde .... *Soprano*
Gunther   *Gibichungs; children of Gibich and*   Grim- *Bass*
Gutrune   *hilde* .... *Soprano*
Hagen—*half brother of Gunther and Gutrune;*
             son of Alberich and Grimhilde .... *Bass*
Waltraute—*a Valkyrie* .... *Mezzo-Soprano*
Alberich .... *Bass*
Woglinde   *Soprano*
Wellgunde *Rhinemaidens* .... *Mezzo-Soprano*
Flosshilde   *Contralto*

Vassals, warriors and women

Der Ring der Nibelungen

It should be clear, if one really thinks about it, that we humans have been singularly blessed by an enormous outpouring of artistic production. So much art exists, in fact, that an individual lifetime is hardly adequate even to begin to grasp it all. But it is also our fate that great art, like anything rich and powerful, can only be properly appreciated by most of us in relatively small doses. Anyone who has ever spent exhausting hours tramping through museums, or has experienced an unremitting day of, say, Beethoven or Brahms or Mozart, or has loved around the clock realizes that there is such a thing as surfeit and that that has nothing whatever to do with intrinsic value.

Wagner's *Ring* cycle is probably a case in point. Although there might be some who would quite honestly profess the keenest of pleasures in the anticipation of a relatively uninterrupted performance of the entire cycle, for most of us less durable mortals such a marathon would probably be purely, simply, and agonizingly too much. On the other hand, the four distinct parts of the opera are usually performed by themselves, either as completely self-sufficient entities or as individual performances separated from each other, presumably, by lengthy and rejuvenating periods of sound sleep for everyone concerned. In such a manner it may be possible to survive the rigors of so much exposure to culture and beauty.

In any event, the *Ring* is monumental, vast, and well-nigh overwhelming in its breadth. The sets alone, involving underwater scenes, fierce storms, great quantities of fire and mist, disappearing acts, goddesses riding steeds through the heavens, and so forth, are sufficiently grand to deter most producers, if not most audiences. Add to this Wagner's music—prodigious in scope and demanding on performers—and the cosmic nature of the theme, and one can become very nearly unhinged by the sheer grandeur of it all.

The underlying theme of the entire cycle of four operas revolves relentlessly around the notion of destiny and the interwoven relations of gods and humans. Set in the ancient German-Scandinavian world where the gods who dwell in Valhalla exhibit, despite the eminence of their exalted status, very clear human weaknesses, there is a constant interplay of the lust for power, the lust for gold, and just plain lust. A

large pile of gold figures prominently, but just why it is so attractive, since its value seems to be more intrinsic than in its power to purchase anything, is unclear. Probably it is merely tradition, somehow, that makes the pure possession of gold so alluring. The golden ring, however, that has the magical property of making its owner—on the condition of renouncing love entirely—lord of all the world, is another matter, and it is the object of desire of gods, humans, and a number of beings apparently somewhere in between.

In their proper order the four parts of the *Ring* cycle are *Das Rheingold, Die Walküre, Siefried* and *Die Götterdämmerung*. The Rhinemaidens, guardians of the gold from which the magical ring is to be made, are early on robbed of their treasure by Alberich, the evil dwarf king of the Nibelungs, and

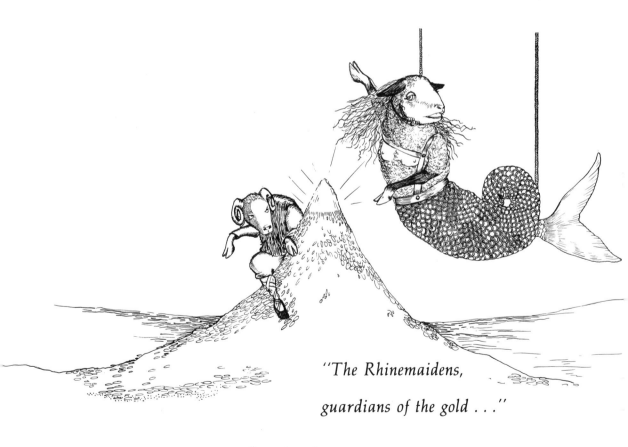

"The Rhinemaidens,

guardians of the gold . . ."

from this point to the end of the cycle, when the ring finally reverts to the Rhinemaidens, there is a constant struggle for its possession. Soon after he has forged the ring, Alberich, much against his will, is relieved of it by Wotan, king of the gods, and he never does get it back, but when Wotan rather dishonorably forces him to give up the ring, Alberich invokes a terrible curse of anguish and death on whoever possesses it. Whether it is the ring and its curse rather than the greed for its possession that causes so much destruction is probably akin to the question of whether wealth itself is as corrupting as is the desire for wealth.

Although the grandiose and complex plot of the cycle involves a number of stories linked together by the persistent, heroic, and futile struggles of humans and gods, it is probably Brünnhilda who is the noblest and most elevated of all the characters who appear in the vast saga. For it is her love for Siegfried and her eventual self-immolation that finally suggest a note of hope for the entire race of humans.

In the first of the two illustrations that we have included for *The Ring*, we see the evil Alberich, who is after the gold that is guarded by the lovely Rhinemaidens. The ropes by which the Rhinemaidens are suspended are not essential elements in the story, although they are rather necessary considering the physical constraints,

"Fafner . . . nearly as formidable as . . . the opera itself . . ."

such as those involved with singing under water—as in the scene depicted here—or floating in air, within which even great opera singers must operate. The Rhinemaidens don't want Alberich to have the gold, although it would seem that they don't really have much practical use for it themselves. Perhaps, however, that suggests something concerning how gold—or power—should always be possessed—as if one really did not want or need it.

The second illustration, from *Siegfried*, the third opera of the *Ring* cycle, depicts the heroic battle between Siegfried and Fafner, the dragon, with Mime, the evil dwarf, looking on malevolently. Fafner is nearly as formidable as is the opera itself, and in a setting that includes Valhalla—seen in the background—as well as the awesome representations of the struggles of gods and humans on the backdrop of nature primeval, he fits in very nicely indeed. Be they human, animal or divine, pure or alloyed in character, there are no torpid types among the characters in *this* story.

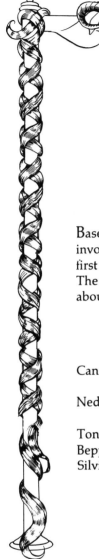

PAGLIACCI

An Opera in Two Acts
by Ruggiero Leoncavallo (1858–1919)
with Libretto by the Composer

Based on the once-familiar Italian pantomimes and comedies involving the characters of Columbine, Harlequin, and Clown; first performed in Teatro dal Verme, Milan, on May 21, 1892. The setting is in Montalto, a province of Calabria in Italy, in about 1865 to 1870. The original language was Italian.

Characters

Canio—*head of a troupe of strolling players; also "Pagliaccio,"*
    the first clown, in the play within the play .... Tenor
Nedda—*wife of Canio; also "Columbine"*
    in the play within the play .... Soprano
Tonio—*a clown, also "Taddeo" in the play* .... Baritone
Beppe—*an actor, also "Harlequin" in the play* .... Tenor
Silvio—*a villager, lover of Nedda* .... Baritone
Villagers and peasants

Pagliacci

Between the sublime and the ridiculous there is but one small step, between love and hate a razor's edge of separation, and between the tragic and the comic no more than the most fragile of demarcations. It is this theme that underlies *Pagliacci*, for the tragic consequences of infidelity and jealous passion unfold on the backdrop of a comic "play-within-a-play."

In the opera, a group of strolling players presents a performance intended to depict the troubles of Pagliaccio with his faithless wife, Columbine, and her lover, Harlequin, in a thoroughly ridiculous and farcical manner, but it so happens that the situation "on stage" is actually a mirror image of the real-life state of the players. Columbine, who offstage is Nedda, the wife of Canio, who plays Pagliaccio, is having an actual affair with Silvio, a wealthy villager, and Canio, aware of her infidelity, is obsessed with his burning desire to know the identity of her lover. He threatens her wildly but to no avail before the play begins, and, finding himself later, during the performance of the play, in a nearly identical position, he departs from the prepared comic lines to demand again the name of his wife's lover. The village audience, initially appreciative of the humor of the play, becomes increasingly uneasy as it becomes evident that an unplanned drama is unfolding upon the stage, a drama that culminates in Canio-Pagliaccio not only stabbing his wife to death as she steadfastly refuses to divulge her lover's name but also plunging his dagger into Silvio's heart as the latter leaps onto the stage in response to Nedda's final gasp, "Soccorso . . . Sil-

"... a hint of pain ...

as there probably always is with clowns ..."

vio! (Help me, Silvio!)" Canio's final words—and the end of the opera—underscore once again the bitter duality of the tragic-comic: "La commedia e finita! (The comedy is ended!)," he sings in anguish.

On the preceding page is depicted a scene from the play-within-a-play, obviously not intended to be a moment of intense seriousness. But there is, nonetheless, a hint of pain on the face of Pagliaccio, as there probably always is with clowns.

MADAM BUTTERFLY

An Opera in Two Acts
by Giacomo Puccini (1858–1924)
with Libretto by Luigi Illica and Giuseppe Giacosa

Based on a story by John Luther Long and a play by David Belasco; first performed at La Scala, Milan, on February 17, 1904. The setting is Nagasaki, Japan, in the nineteenth century. The original language was Italian.

Characters

Madam Butterfly (Cio-Cio-San) .... *Soprano*
Suzuki—*servant to Cio-Cio-San* .... *Mezzo-Soprano*
Kate Pinkerton—*Lieutenant Pinkerton's American wife*
.... *Mezzo-Soprano*
B. F. Pinkerton—*Lieutenant, United States Navy* .... *Tenor*
Sharpless—*American Consul at Nagasaki* .... *Baritone*
Goro—*a marriage broker* .... *Tenor*
Prince Yamadori—*a wealthy Japanese suitor of Cio-Cio-San*
.... *Baritone*
The Bonze—*Cio-Cio-San's uncle and a Buddhist Priest* ...... *Bass*
The Imperial Commissioner .... *Bass*
The Official Registrar .... *Baritone*
Trouble—*Cio-Cio-San's child*
      Cio-Cio-San's relatives and friends; servants

Madam Butterfly

Unlike so much tragic opera—as well as nonmusical drama—which depend for their effects upon misunderstandings, mistaken identities and so forth, *Madam Butterfly* needs no such quirkish turns of fate to achieve its poignancy. There is no evil brother or stepfather or guardian to work his deceptions, nor is there even a protagonist who is clearly an evil-doer. There is merely Lieutenant Pinkerton, United States Navy, whose major shortcoming is more a matter of a lack of depth than anything smacking of true malevolence. Yet this is enough, when it encounters the loyalty and steadfastness of the lovely Cio-Cio-San—Madam Butterfly—to set in motion the train of events that is to lead to heartbreak and tragedy.

Madam Butterfly is authentically Japanese in tone, and some of its musical themes are unquestionably of Japanese origin. The action takes place in Nagasaki, the city fated to have its name immortalized nearly a century later with far broader connotations than those of Cio-Cio-San. Perhaps it is Lieutenant Pinkerton's shallowness of character, perhaps his unconscious perpetuation of the American conviction—hopefully less common now than formerly—of the natural inferiority of Orientals, that causes him to enter casually into a marriage contract with Cio-Cio-San without realizing that her love for him is so profound that she excludes everything else from her life and mind, even her reverence for her traditional deities. At any rate, Pinkerton, knowing full well that he will find an American girl to be his "real" wife, marries Madam Butterfly, and there are moments, it must be said,

". . . the lovely Cio-Cio-San—Madam Butterfly . . ."

when a genuine rapture and love exists between them.

Pinkerton is absent at sea for three years after his marriage to Cio-Cio-San, during which time she bears his beautiful son, destined, so she sings, someday so to captivate the Emperor that he will make him a prince, and she never wavers in her devotion to her husband and in her belief that he will return—as he promised—when the robins nest in the spring. She sings a touching aria, in which she describes the happiness she anticipates when his ship returns.

Cio-Cio-San's innocence and her unhesitating faith in Pinkerton are proof even against the knowledge of his infidelity that her friends try to communicate to her, unswerving even in the face of a letter from Pinkerton, announcing that he has an American wife, that the American Consul, Sharpless, tries in vain to read to her. When Pinkerton finally returns, Cio-Cio-San joyfully prepares for his arrival, and it is only when she is faced with his new wife, Kate, that she finally accepts—with extraordinary dignity—her betrayal. Kate, no shrew, implores her forgiveness, and even Pinkerton, no scoundrel at heart, is aghast at the final scene when he sees that Cio-Cio-San, giving up her beloved child to him, has stabbed herself with her ceremonial sword that has inscribed upon it, "Death with honor is better than life without honor."

There are lighthearted moments in the opera, charming in their delicacy and bittersweet in their contrast with the inevitable direction that one knows the opera is taking. But its central and most poignant element is embodied in the character of Cio-Cio-San herself, in her simple but profound dignity and in the complete selflessness of her steadfast loyalty. Pictured on the preceding page, we see her in a typical costume, with her lute, on which she was wont to play at happy moments, beside her.

PART THREE

The Twentieth Century

It is tempting to suggest that the hallmark of twentieth-century opera or, perhaps, of art in general during that period, is realism, but it may be somewhat more accurate to say that its direction is away from romanticism and the lushness of over-stated sentiment and towards a kind of spare objectivity that expresses the variety of the human condition in essentially life-like and graphic terms. But probably the most accurate statement would be to say that all categorization is dangerous and that the most that can be truly discerned in the history of art are movements that are never clearly delineated, never without exceptions, and always complex.

In any case, we have included four twentieth-century operas in our collection and, again, while they are hardly completely representative of modern trends in operatic composition, they are sufficiently different from their older counterparts to justify their placement in a category of their own.

Here, then, are the concluding elements of our brief look at opera, and if the reader is still experiencing difficulties in handling our fairly preposterous muttons, perhaps he should at least be grateful that we launched our assault on only seventeen operas; we could, after all, have decided to assail considerably more.

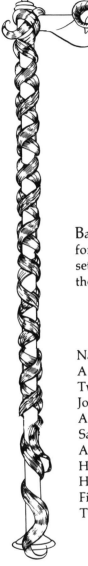
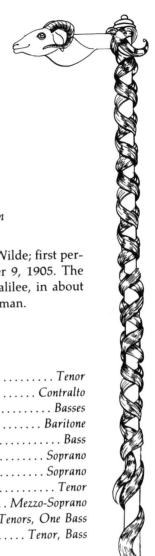

SALOME

An Opera in One Act
by Richard Strauss (1864–1949)
with Libretto by Hedwig Lachmann

Based on the dramatic poem, *Salome*, by Oscar Wilde; first performed at the Hofoper, Dresden, on December 9, 1905. The setting is the palace of Herod at Tiberias in Galilee, in about the year 30 A.D. The original language was German.

Characters

Narraboth—*a young Syrian Captain of the Guard* .... Tenor
A Page to Herodias .... Contralto
Two Soldiers .... Basses
Jochanaan—*John the Baptist* .... Baritone
A Cappadocian .... Bass
Salome—*daughter of Herodias* .... Soprano
A Slave .... Soprano
Herod Antipas—*Tetrarch of Judea* .... Tenor
Herodias—*Herod's wife, mother of Salome* .... Mezzo-Soprano
Five Jews .... Four Tenors, One Bass
Two Nazarenes .... Tenor, Bass
Executioner

Salome

Strauss's grisly opera, *Salome*, is a study of the encounter of psychological degeneracy with thundering religious zeal. It is the story of John the Baptist, whose preaching about moral reformation and the advent of the one mightier than he who is to come after him has resulted in his incarceration by Herod, the ruler of Judea.

Herod is weak, decadent, and debased, and so, in the main, are all those around him, principally his new wife, Herodias, who has murdered her former husband in order to marry him, and her daughter, Salome, a beautiful but thoroughly conscienceless wretch for whom Herod openly lusts, much to Herodias's discomfiture. The voice of John the Baptist issues from his underground cell in fulminating denunciations of the sinners who are disporting themselves in Herod's banquet hall, but while his words and awesome pronouncements strike fear into the hearts of most who hear them, Salome is moved in a different way. She lusts for him in a most fierce fashion, and when he is brought before her, she openly expresses her desire for his body, his hair, his lips. A young Syrian Captain, hopelessly smitten by her beauty, kills himself at her feet in anguish over her lechery, but Salome does not so much as glance at him. John declares that she is cursed, as he retreats into his cell, while Salome's only reaction is a continued frenzy of carnal appetite.

Herod, obsessed with his desire for Salome, entreats her to dance, and she finally performs for him the famous dance of the seven veils, in which she progressively sheds her veils in what certainly must be one of the earliest examples of

". . . with a horrible triumph . . ."

an art form familiar in some circles even today. But Salome has extracted from Herod his royal promise to grant her any wish she desires, and when she finishes her dance, it is—partly because of her fury at the Prophet's rejection of her advances and partly because of her mother's suggestion—the head of John the Baptist on a silver platter for which she asks.

It must be admitted that Herod, either because of his terrified awe of John or because of some minuscule vestige of moral sense, does his best to avoid the granting of Salome's wish, but she is adamant, and—as is depicted in the accompanying illustration—it is with a horrible triumph that she accepts the severed head of the Prophet as it is presented to her. Even Herod is revolted and horrified by this, and he orders Salome's death. She is crushed to death beneath the shields of his soldiers, as the curtain falls.

Strauss, like numerous other operatic composers, particularly Wagner, who influenced him strongly, employed the technique of identifying a unique and repeated musical phrase with the various characters in his drama. An association develops, therefore, during the course of a performance that immeasurably strengthens the intimate relationship of dramatic action and musical background, and it is this relationship that is really to a large extent what opera is all about in the first place.

Salome shocked its first audiences, and it is probable that despite our modern resistance to shock—possibly through our repeated exposure to it—we are still at least somewhat disquieted by the opera's naked revelation of the depths of human degradation. It is not the greatest of operas nor the most profound, but it is without question one of the most vivid of excursions into the world of neurasthenic and pathological impairment amidst the intensity of human desires and the severity of religious calls for redemption.

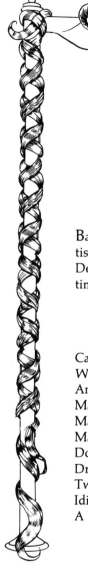
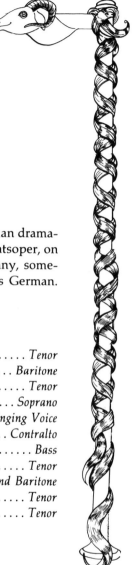

WOZZECK

An Opera in Three Acts
by Alban Berg (1885–1935)
with Libretto by the Composer

Based on the dramatic tragedy, *Wozzeck*, by the German dramatist, Georg Büchner; first performed at the Berlin Staatsoper, on December 14, 1925. The setting is a town in Germany, sometime after World War I. The original language was German.

Characters

Captain .... *Tenor*
Wozzeck—*a soldier* .... *Baritone*
Andres—*a friend of Wozzeck* .... *Tenor*
Marie—*mistress of Wozzeck* .... *Soprano*
Marie's Baby Son .... *Singing Voice*
Margret—*neighbor of Marie* .... *Contralto*
Doctor .... *Bass*
Drum Major .... *Tenor*
Two Apprentices .... *Bass and Baritone*
Idiot .... *Tenor*
A Soldier .... *Tenor*
Soldiers, maids, children, servants

Wozzeck

Wozzeck was completed in 1921 and was given its first performance more than four years later in Berlin. From the beginning, the opera has evoked controversy and has been polarizing in its effects. The wide extremes of audience reaction undoubtedly have stemmed from the fact that Berg, following the lead of his mentor, Schoenberg, composed the opera in atonal form. To the musician this suggests the twelve-tone scale, the discarding of key signatures, the dissociation of melody, harmony, and conventional musical structure. To the nonmusician this often means cacophony, disorder, and the vague stirrings of an impotent rage. To the ignorant it probably means nothing at all, but, then, to them there is not much beyond the hopelessly rudimentary that can ever really mean very much.

In any case, Wozzeck departed radically from practically all hitherto accepted musical and operatic tradition. There are no arias and none of the individual or ensemble singing normally associated with opera; rather, vocalizing is often, although certainly not exclusively, in the form of "sprechstimme," a kind of declamation with a musical background that is more akin to the reading of poetry, with its well-defined rhythm and intonation, than with conventional singing. It should be pointed out, however, that the music of composers such as Schoenberg and Berg is no more lacking in form and structure than is "modern" art; the fact that the form is unfamiliar and complex does not imply that the music is without form or that it is meaningless. On the other hand, there may be a bit of doubt as to the meaning of meaning when there is no understanding whatever, even—one sometimes cannot help wondering—in an artist's mind.

*". . . Wozzeck's child, astride his hobbyhorse . . . totally unaware
. . ."*

Dramatically, the opera is grimly and relentlessly tragic, and although there are moments of humor, there is little, if any, lightness, and the overall philosophical tone is that of a depressing commentary on the generally worthless condition of humanity. Wozzeck, himself, is an archetypal common man and a soldier, one whose doom lies not only in his nature but also in the collective natures of the ignoble human beings in his life. He is deceived by Marie, his mistress and the mother of his child, used by a quack doctor in valueless experiments, and treated with contempt by his superior officer. He is obsessed by visions of blood and death, and when he cuts Marie's throat because of her infidelity and later drowns himself in a totally distracted frame of mind, one feels more that nature is taking its grimly proper course than that there is any kind of resolution to the human dilemma.

There is probably no more potent dramatic means of intensifying a depiction of tragedy and horror than by juxtaposing it with simplicity and innocence. A Sydney Carton going to the guillotine transfixes us with a sense of the tragic, but one knows, nonetheless, that he is fully aware of what is happening. Children, on the other hand, moving wide-eyed and benightedly towards their dooms, the little princes, for example, in the Tower of London innocently awaiting their executions, stir within us an agony whose sharpness is given another dimension by the essential irony of the situation. In the final scene of *Wozzeck,* the scene shown on the preceding page, we are presented with a picture of Wozzeck's child, astride his hobbyhorse and totally unaware of the cruel and grisly events that have swirled about him. It is a supremely ironic scene and serves to underscore with an immense poignancy the dismaying message of the entire opera.

In the final analysis, life may, of course, not be totally appalling, but the judgment is one that all of us must draw for ourselves from what ever indications we may see, including, presumably, *Wozzeck.*

AMAHL AND THE NIGHT VISITORS

An Opera in One Act
by Gian Carlo Menotti (1911–   )
with Libretto by the Composer

Based on the Christian Nativity story; first performed by the NBC Television Opera Theater in New York City on Christmas Eve 1951, and—as a stage première—on April 19, 1952, by the New York City Opera Company. The setting is that of legendary antiquity at the time of the birth of Christ. The original language was English.

Characters

Amahl—*a crippled child of about twelve* .... *Boy Soprano*
Amahl's Mother .... *Soprano*
The Page .... *Bass*
King Kaspar (*slightly deaf*) .... *Tenor*
King Balthazar .... *Bass*
King Melchior .... *Baritone*
Shepherds and villagers

Amahl and the Night
Visitors

A*mahl*, expressly commissioned for television, was first performed by the NBC Television Opera Theatre on Christmas Eve in 1951, and it has become over subsequent years a traditional television favorite during Christmas seasons. But much in the same way that the meaning of Christmas transcends time and season, the humor, charm, and profoundly moving nature of Menotti's exquisite opera speak to ideas and feelings that are universal in scope and that touch the very essence of all that the word humanity suggests.

Purely from a dramatic point of view, there can be little question that one of the most effective achievements of any artist must be the subtle and incredibly delicate balancing of humor and pathos in such a way that an audience finds itself in the grip, alternately, of both laughter and tears. In this regard *Amahl* succeeds probably as well as any work of art ever has, particularly because there is no hint of artificiality or of the use of dramatic devices; rather, the emotional responses of the audience come completely naturally and are the result of an unavoidable identification with the humanity of the characters in the opera and with the sensitivity of the music.

The story centers around the crippled shepherd boy Amahl, and his widowed mother. Living in abject poverty, they happen, one bitterly cold night, to be brief hosts to the three kings of antiquity, who, following the star and bearing gifts, are seeking the infant Christ child. The kings are devout, sincere, and gentle, and one of them—as Amahl excitedly tells his unbelieving mother—is black. In addition, an-

"... *Amahl's gift, no longer needed for its primal purpose* ..."

other—Kaspar—suffers a hearing defect that is sufficiently pronounced to cause him constantly to be asking for speeches to be repeated. The gifts they bear are rich and of great value, but all that Amahl can offer to send to the child is the crutch that he has made, which is for him, of course, invaluable. As he offers the crutch, he miraculously finds that he can walk unaided, and it would be a hard heart indeed that could be witness to this most poignant evidence of the power of self-less love without being deeply moved.

The music of the opera is melodic, sparkling, and of immense charm, and it is in such harmony with the story and the characters that one almost feels that the tale could not be told without it. Utterly without pretense, devoid of any striv-ings for effect, it is a part of a whole that comes very close to a gemlike artistic perfection.

The climactic point of the opera is, of course, the scene in which Amahl, having made the spontaneous gesture of his great gift, takes his first few halting steps without his crutch. The three kings, not slow to recognize the miracle that has occurred, break into joyous cries of, "He walks! He walks!," and the opera draws to a close as they prepare to continue their journey, accompanied now by Amahl, who—probably not unlike any child of any century—must first endure the admonitions of his mother regarding how he must behave on his trip. The illustration on the preceding page is of Amahl and the three kings as they leave on their journey to the man-ger. Please note that Amahl's gift, no longer needed for its primal purpose, is now being carried by a camel, together, presumably, with its less valuable companions, the gold, frankincense, myrrh and—if Menotti is to be believed—lico-rice of the three kings. If Amahl appears a bit stunned, it may be because of his tender age and the high excitement of being a key figure in one of the most epic moments of human his-tory.

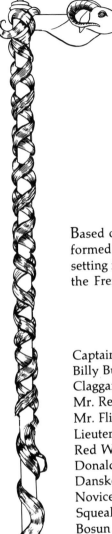

BILLY BUDD

An Opera in Four Acts
by Benjamin Britten (1913–1976)
with Libretto by E. M. Forster and Eric Crozier

Based on the story, *Billy Budd*, by Herman Melville; first performed at Covent Garden, London, on December 1, 1951. The setting is aboard H.M.S. Indomitable, a British warship, during the French wars of 1797. The original language was English.

Characters

Captain Vere—*commanding H.M.S.* Indomitable .... *Tenor*
Billy Budd—*an impressed seaman* .... *Baritone*
Claggart—*Master-at-arms* .... *Bass*
Mr. Redburn—*First Lieutenant* .... *Baritone*
Mr. Flint—*Sailing Master* .... *Baritone*
Lieutenant Ratcliffe .... *Bass*
Red Whiskers—*an impressed sailor* .... *Tenor*
Donald—*a member of the crew* .... *Baritone*
Dansker—*an old seaman* .... *Bass*
Novice .... *Tenor*
Squeak—*ship's corporal* .... *Tenor*
Bosun .... *Baritone*
First and Second Mates .... *Baritones*
Maintop .... *Tenor*
The Novice's Friend .... *Baritone*
Arthur Jones—*an impressed sailor* .... *Baritone*
Four Midshipmen .... *Boys' Voices*
    Officers, sailors, powder monkeys, drummers, marines

Billy Budd

Herman Melville's tale of Billy Budd, the handsome sailor, Adam before the fall, is, of course, not only a classic in the annals of sea literature but is probably also among the greatest of all tales ever told in any genre. It is well-nigh universal in scope, possessing an appeal on a great number of levels, from that of simply being an engrossing story to that of being a disquisition on the philosophical relations of good and evil. It touches on the most elemental problems, dilemmas, and uncertainties of humanity, and its setting is the sea, the most elemental of nature's stages.

Benjamin Britten based his opera on Melville's story, and the libretto—written in prose rather than verse—is largely the work of the great English novelist, E. M. Forster. While there are several details of the opera that either depart from Melville's account or that bear a somewhat different emphasis, the basic ideas are the same. Billy represents the purity and innocence of man prior to original sin, a perfection untouched by the ameliorating influences of civilization, an Adam, whose defense against evil lies like a primal blessing in his inability to recognize it. Billy has not eaten of the apple, and it is precisely for this reason that evil does not exist for him and—above all—cannot touch him. Claggart, the Master-at-Arms on Billy's ship, is, on the other hand, the embodiment, the essence of evil. It is not so much that Claggart is a corrupt man as it is that he is a perfect Satan. Evil is for him as much the breath of life as is goodness for Billy.

Clearly, as Melville put it, something must come of their confrontation. Claggart almost loves Billy—there are unmistakable Freudian overtones in his reactions to him—but at the same time, in a way that is not really contradictory, he sees in him his greatest opportunity, his ultimate chal-

"Billy . . . standing

beneath the mast from which he must eventually hang . . ."

lenge: what, after all, could be more at the essence of Satanic evil than the destruction of a perfect goodness? But Satan, as always, requires an entrance, an invitation, a flaw, and Billy, who *is* human, *does* have "Satan's little card." In moments of stress, he stammers, the words will not come to his lips, and it is in the presence of his Captain, "Starry" Vere, that Billy, accused totally without foundation of inciting mutiny and unable to defend himself verbally, lashes out and with one blow kills the Master-at-Arms. Claggart has won, and in his death has achieved his most fervent desire.

Captain Vere is a man of paramount importance and interest in the story. He is introspective, scholarly, articulate, and compassionate, but he is also the dedicated and unswerving servant of the King. He knows that Billy is an angel of God, but he also knows that the angel must die. His is the impossible choice but the unavoidable decision, and when Billy is hanged from the yardarm, Vere knows full well that the Adam has become the crucified Christ.

Britten's opera begins with Vere, an old man long retired, meditating on his life and his place in the perpetual struggle of good and evil, and ends with the aged Vere once again reliving his Pilate-like role. But Billy's last utterance as he ascends by the rope from the yardarm is to bless Captain Vere, and if the agony of Christ on the cross represents hope for fallible sinful humanity, so, too, does Billy's immolation represent the possibility of redemption for Vere, as for all men, and of the ultimate triumph of good over evil.

On the preceding page we are on the deck of H.M.S. *Indomitable.* In the background is the introspective Captain Vere, undoubtedly meditating on life and the meaning of things in general. Billy is in the foreground, standing beneath the mast from which he must eventually hang. On the right we recognize Claggart as he is, a true wolf among sheep, but it would be a distinct mistake to assume from Billy's gesture that he has even a glimmering of such a recognition.

A Curtain Call

Not the least part of the spectacle of opera is its association with the theaters where it has been performed over the years. Some of these, which double as sites for other types of stage productions, have no character specifically relating them to opera. But there are a number that were built exclusively for opera, and in many cases their names and their magnificence have become inextricably and exclusively linked to opera.

La Scala in Milan, Vienna's State Opéra House, the Royal Opera House in London, the Théâtre Nationale de l'Opera in Paris, the Metropolitan Opera House in New York are but a few whose names almost immediately conjure up visions of operas and opera stars, both bygone and current. They are as synonymous with opera as are names such as Caruso, Albanese, Callas, Chaliapin, Farrar, Fisher-Dieskau, Flagstad, Lehmann, Lind, Melba, Melchior, Nilsson, Pavarotti, Peerce, Peters, Pinza, Pons, Ponselle, Sayao, Schwarz-